MW01592560

This Notebook Belongs To

____

Made in the USA
Monee, IL
11 December 2019

18382058R00072